Teach Me...
Everyday
JAPANESE
Volume 1

Written by Judy Mahoney

Illustrated by Patrick Girouard

Technology is changing our world. Far away exotic places have literally become neighbors. We belong to a global community and our children are becoming "global kids." Comparing and understanding different languages and cultures is more vital than ever! Additionally, learning a foreign language reinforces a child's overall education. Early childhood is the optimal time for children to learn a second language, and the Teach Me Everyday language series is a practical and inspiring way to teach them. Through story and song, each book and audio encourages them to listen, speak, read and write in a foreign language.

Today's "global kids" hold tomorrow's world in their hands. So when it comes to learning a new language, don't be surprised when they say, "teach me!"

The Japanese language has two kinds of alphabet: Hiragana and Katakana. The Japanese alphabet consists of 99 sounds formed with five vowels (a, e, i, o and u) and fourteen consonants (k, s, t, h, m, y, r, w, g, z, d, b, p and n). Transliteration is a process that uses Roman letters to phonetically sound out characters. In Japanese, transliterations are called romaji.

Teach Me Everyday Japanese
Volume One
ISBN 13: 978-1-59972-104-0
Library of Congress PCN: 2008902658

Copyright © 2008 by Teach Me Tapes, Inc.
6016 Blue Circle Drive, Minnetonka, MN 55343
www.teachmetapes.com

Book Design by Design Lab, Northfield, MN

10 9 8 7 6 5 4 3 2

INDEX & SONG LIST

Minna de Utaeba ♪

Minna de utaeba, utaeba, utaeba
Minna de utaeba, tanoshiku naru ne
Anata mo watashi mo
Minna tomodachi
Minna de utaeba, tanoshiku naru ne.

The More We Get Together
The more we get together, together, together
The more we get together the happier we'll be
For your friends are my friends
And my friends are your friends
The more we get together the happier we'll be.

こんにちは。
わたしのなまえはまり。
あなたのなまえはなに?
Konnichiwa. Watashi no namae wa Mari. Anata no namae wa nani?

わたしのかぞくをしょうかいします。
おかあさんとおとうさん
おとうと、そしてわたし。
Watashi no kazoku o shookai shimasu. Okaasan Otoosan Otooto, soshite Watashi.

Hello. My name is Mari. What is your name?

I will introduce my family: my mother, my father, my younger brother and me.

おとうと
Otooto

おとうさん
Otoosan

おかあさん
Okaasan

わたし
Watashi

My father
My brother
My mother
Me

ご
go

5

うちのねこ。
なまえはたま。
いろははいいろ。
Uchi no neko.
Namae wa Tama.
Iro wa haiiro.

My cat.
His name is Tama.
His color is gray.

うちのねこ
Uchi no neko

うちのいぬ。
なまえはポチ。
いろはくろとしろ。
Uchi no inu.
Namae wa Pochi.
Iro wa kuro to shiro.

うちのいぬ
Uchi no inu

My dog.
His name is Pochi.
His color is black and white.

これはわたしのいえです。
やねはちゃいろで にわには
きいろいはながさいて いるの。

Kore wa watashi no ie desu.
Yane wa chairo de
niwa ni wa kiiroi hana ga
saiteiru no.

This is my house.
The roof is brown
and in the garden
yellow flowers bloom.

わたしのへやのいろはあお。
もうしちじだわ。さあ、おきましょう!
おきましょう!

Watashi no heya no iro wa ao.
Moo shichi-ji da wa.
Saa, okimashoo!
Okimashoo!

The color of my room is
blue. It is seven o'clock.
Now it's time to get up!
Now it's time to get up!

Yaoya-san

Yaoya-san no omise ni naranda
Shinamono mite goran
Yoku mite goran kangaete goran
Tomato tomato.

Mada Neteru no

Mada neteru no, mada neteru no
Onii-san, onii-san
Kyookai no kane ga
    natteiru no ni
Kin-kon-kan, kin-kon-kan.

The Vegetable Shop
Look at all the vegetables
Lined up at the vegetable shop
Look at them carefully and think
Tomato, tomato.

Are You Sleeping
Are you sleeping, are you sleeping
Brother John, Brother John
Morning bells are ringing
Morning bells are ringing
Ding dang dong! Ding dang dong!

きゅう
kyuu

9

Today is Monday.
Do you know the days of the week?
Monday, Tuesday, Wednesday,
Thursday, Friday, Saturday, Sunday.

げつようび
Getsu yoobi

Monday

かようび
Ka yoobi

Tuesday

すいようび
Sui yoobi

Wednesday

もくようび
Moku yoobi

Thursday

きんようび
Kin yoobi

Friday

どようび
Do yoobi

Saturday

にちようび
Nichi yoobi

Sunday

じゅういち
juu-ichi

11

ようふくをきましょう。
ブラウスをきて、
ズボンとくつをはいて、
ぼうしをかぶります。
Yoohuku o kimashoo.
Burausu o kite, zubon to,
kutsu o haite, booshi o
kaburimasu.

Let's get dressed.
I put on my blouse,
my pants, my shoes
and my hat.

Atama, Kata, Hiza, Ashi ♪ ♪

Atama kata, hiza ashi, hiza ashi
Atama kata, hiza ashi, hiza ashi
Me to mimi to kuchi to hana
Atama kata, hiza ashi, hiza ashi.

Head, Shoulders, Knees and Toes
Head and shoulders, knees and toes, knees and toes
Head and shoulders, knees and toes, knees and toes
Eyes and ears and mouth and nose
Head and shoulders, knees and toes, knees and toes.

I eat breakfast. Breakfast is rice, soup and fried eggs. I also drink tea.

そとはあめです。
きょうはさんぽにいけません。
Soto wa ame desu.
Kyoo wa sanpo ni ikemasen.

It is raining outside.
I cannot go for a walk today.

Ame Ame Itchae

Ame ame itchae
Mata ato de kite yo
Ame ame itchae
Booya ga soto de asobenai.

Niji

Ao ya midori
Tottemo kireena iro
Pinku ni murasaki kiiro
Niji ni notte mitai.

Rain Medley

Rain, rain, go away
Come again another day
Rain, rain, go away
Little Johnny wants to play.

It's raining, it's pouring
The old man is snoring
He bumped his head and went to bed
And couldn't get up in the morning.

Rainbows

Sometimes blue and sometimes green
Prettiest colors I've ever seen
Pink and purple, yellow - whee!
I love to ride those rainbows.

ここはわたしのがっこう。
まいあさ「せんせい、おはようございます」ってあいさつします。 そして、すうじとひらがなのおさらいをします。
Koko wa watashi no gakkoo.
Maiasa "Sensee, Ohayoo gozaimasu" tte aisatsu shimasu. Soshite, suuji to hiragana no osarai o shimasu.

わたしのがっこう
Watashi no gakkoo

Here is my school. Every morning
I say, "Good morning, teacher."
I review the numbers and the alphabet.

すうじ (Suuji)

1	2	3	4	5	6	7	8	9	10
いち ichi	に ni	さん san	よん yon	ご go	ろく roku	なな nana	はち hachi	きゅう kyuu	じゅう juu

ごじゅうおん (Gojuuon)

あ (a)　い (i)　う (u)　え (e)　お (o)　か (ka)　き (ki)

く (ku)　け (ke)　こ (ko)　さ (sa)　し (shi)　す (su)　せ (se)　そ (so)

た (ta)　ち (chi)　つ (tsu)　て (te)　と (to)　な (na)　に (ni)　ぬ (nu)

ね (ne)　の (no)　は (ha)　ひ (hi)　ふ (fu)　へ (he)　ほ (ho)　ま (ma)

み (mi)　む (mu)　め (me)　も (mo)　や (ya)　ゆ (yu)　よ (yo)　ら (ra)

り (ri)　る (ru)　れ (re)　ろ (ro)　わ (wa)　を (o)　ん (n)

AIUEO

A i u e o ka ki ku ke ko
Dareka ga dokoka de naratteru
Sa shi su se so ta chi tsu te to
Dareka ga dokoka de hanashiteru
Na ni nu ne no ha hi hu he ho
Dareka ga dokoka de wasureteru

Ma mi mu me mo ya i yu e yo
Dareka ga dokoka de utatteru
Ra ri ru re ro wa i u e o
Dareka ga dokoka de dokoka de
Dareka ga donatteru n.

The Alphabet Song
(The Japanese alphabet is woven into these verses.)

Someone is learning
　　somewhere
Someone is talking
　　somewhere
Someone is forgetting
　　somewhere
Someone is singing
　　somewhere
Someone is yelling
　　somewhere.

Merii-san no Hitsuji

Merii-san no hitsuji mee-mee hitsuji
Merii-san no hitsuji masshiro ne
Doko de mo tsuiteiku mee-mee tsuiteiku
Doko de mo tsuiteiku kawaii ne.

Mary Had a Little Lamb
Mary had a little lamb, little lamb, little lamb
Mary had a little lamb, its fleece was white as snow
Everywhere that Mary went, Mary went, Mary went
Everywhere that Mary went the lamb was sure to go.

Ittoo no Zoo-san

Ni-too no zoo-san yattekita
Kumonosu no ue de asobooto
Tottemo tanoshikatta no de
Nakamao ittoo yobimashita.

San-too...
Yon-too...
Go-too...

One Elephant
One elephant went out to play
Upon a spider's web one day
He had such enormous fun
That he called for another elephant to come.

Two elephants . . .
Three elephants . . .
Four elephants . . .
Five elephants . . .

Te o Tatakimashoo

Te o tatakimashoo, tan-tan-tan, tan-tan-tan
Ashibumi shimashoo, tan-tan-tan-tan, tan-tan-tan.

Waraimashoo wa-ha-ha
Waraimashoo wa-ha-ha
Wa ha ha, wa ha ha
Aa omoshiroi!

Te o tatakimashoo, tan-tan-tan, tan-tan-tan
Ashibumi shimashoo, tan-tan-tan-tan, tan-tan-tan.

Okorimashoo un-un-un
Okorimashoo un-un-un
Un-un-un, un-un-un
Aa omoshiroi!

Te o tatakimashoo, tan-tan-tan, tan-tan-tan
Ashibumi shimashoo, tan-tan-tan-tan, tan-tan-tan.

Nakimashoo en-en-en
Nakimashoo en-en-en
En-en-en, en-en-en
Aa omoshiroi!

Let's Clap Hands

Chorus:
Let's clap hands, clap clap clap,
    clap clap clap
Let's stamp feet, stamp stamp stamp,
    stamp stamp stamp.

Let's laugh, ha-ha-ha
Let's laugh, ha-ha-ha
Ha-ha-ha, ha-ha-ha
Oh, it's fun!

Chorus

Let's get angry, unh-unh-unh
Let's get angry, unh-unh-unh
Unh-unh-unh, unh-unh-unh
Oh, it's fun!

Chorus

Let's cry, wah-wah-wah
Let's cry, wah-wah-wah
Wah-wah-wah, wah-wah-wah
Oh, it's fun!

Kuruma no Taiya

Kuruma no taiya wa kuru-kuru
Kuru-kuru, kuru-kuru
Kuruma no taiya wa kuru-kuru
Machi no naka.

Kurakushon wa bu-bu-bu
Bu-bu-bu, bu-bu-bu
Kurakushon wa bu-bu-bu
Machi no naka.

Kodomotachi wa "Saa tabeyoo"
"Hirugohan, saa tabeyoo"
Kodomotachi wa "Saa tabeyoo"
Machi no naka.

The Wheels on the Car

The wheels on the car go round and round
Round and round, round and round
The wheels on the car go round and round
All around the town.

The horn on the car goes beep beep beep
Beep beep beep, beep beep beep
The horn on the car goes beep beep beep
All around the town.

The children in the car go,
"Let's have lunch, let's have lunch,
    let's have lunch"
The children in the car go, "Let's have lunch"
All around the town.

さあひるごはんです。
ひるごはんのあとは、
おひるねします。

Saa hiru gohan desu.
Hiru gohan no ato wa
ohirune shimasu.

It is lunch time.
After lunch we take a nap.

Shizukani Me o Tojite

Shizukani me o tojite
Papa ga kanariya o kattageyoo
Utao o wasureta torinaraba
Daiya no yubiwa o kattageyoo
Daiya ga shinchuu ni kawattara
Kagami o kattageyoo
Kagami ga kowarete mo
Booya wa ichiban kawaii ko.

Hush Little Baby
Hush little baby don't say a word
Papa's going to buy you a mockingbird
If that mockingbird won't sing
Papa's going to buy you a diamond ring
If that diamond ring turns brass
Papa's going to buy you a looking glass
If that looking glass falls down
You'll still be the sweetest little baby in town.

おひるねのあとは、こうえんへいきます。
あひるがいるわね。ともだちといっしょに
はしのうえでうたったりおどったりするの。

*Ohirune no ato wa, kooen e ikimasu.
Ahiru ga iru wa ne. Tomodachi to issho
ni hashi no ue de utattari
odottari suru no.*

After our naps, we go to the park.
I see the ducks. I sing and dance
with my friends on the bridge.

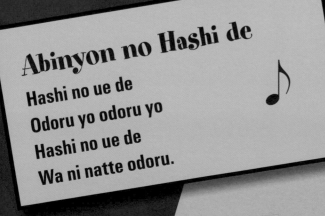

Abinyon no Hashi de

Hashi no ue de
Odoru yo odoru yo
Hashi no ue de
Wa ni natte odoru.

On the Bridge of Avignon
On the bridge of Avignon
They're all dancing, they're all dancing
On the bridge of Avignon
They're all dancing round and round.

Sakura Sakura

Sakura sakura
Noyamamo satomo
Miwatasu kagiri
Kasumi ka kumo ka
Asahi ni niou
Sakura sakura hanazakari.

Rokuwa no Ahiru

Rokuwa no ahiru ga imashita
Futotcho ni yaseppochi iroiro
Demo haneno aru ahiru ga
Sentoo ni natte kwa-kwa-kwa
Kwa-kwa-kwa, kwa-kwa-kwa
Sentoo ni natte kwa-kwa-kwa
Kwa-kwa-kwa, kwa-kwa-kwa.

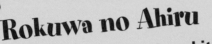

The Cherry Blossom Song

Cherry blossoms, cherry blossoms
On mountains, in villages
As far as you can see
They look like fog or clouds
They are fragrant in the morning sun
Cherry blossoms, cherry blossoms
In full bloom.

Six Little Ducks

Six little ducks that I once knew
Fat ones, skinny ones, fair ones, too
But the one little duck
With the feather on his back
He led the others with his
Quack quack quack
Quack quack quack
Quack quack quack
He led the others with his
Quack quack quack.

にじゅうご
nijuu-go

25

おなかがす
いたわね。そう、ばん
ごはんのじかんです。
Onaka ga suita wa ne.
Soo ban gohan no
jikan desu.

I am hungry.
It is dinner time.

Oo! Suzanna

Watasha Arabama kara
Ruijiana e
Banjoo o motte dekaketa tokoro desu
Oo! Suzanna nakunojanai
Banjoo o motte dekaketa tokoro desu.

Oh! Susanna
Well, I come from Alabama
With a banjo on my knee
I'm going to Louisiana, my true love for to see
Oh, Susanna, won't you cry for me
'Cause I come from Alabama
With a banjo on my knee.

もうよるです。
そらにほしがみえますか。
Moo yoru desu.
Sora ni hoshi ga
miemasu ka.

It's night time. Can you see the stars in the sky?

Ohoshi-sama

Ohoshi-sama hikaru
Ittai anata wa dare deshoo
Osora no ue de
Ohanashi shiteru
Ohoshi-sama hikaru
Ittai anata wa dare deshoo.

Twinkle, Twinkle
Twinkle, twinkle, little star
How I wonder what you are
Up above the world so high
Like a diamond in the sky
Twinkle, twinkle, little star
How I wonder what you are.

Komori Uta

Nen-nen kororiyo okororiyo
Booya wa yoiko da nenneshina
Booya no omori wa doko e itta
Ano yama koete
Sato e itta
Satono miyage ni nani moratta
Den den daiko ni
Shoo no hue.

Japanese Lullaby
Night, night, baby, go to sleep
You are a good baby, go to sleep
Where did your babysitter go?
She went home to the other side
Of the mountain
What did she bring you?
She brought a little rattle-drum
And a flute.

おかあさん、おやすみなさい。
おとうさん、おやすみなさい。
みなさん、おやすみなさい。

Okaasan, oyasuminasai.
Otoosan, oyasuminasai.
Minasan, oyasuminasai.
Oyasuminasai.

Goodnight, Mother.
Goodnight, Father.
Goodnight everyone.
Goodnight.

Oyasuminasai Minasan

Oyasuminasai Minasan
Oyasuminasai Minasan
Oyasuminasai Minasan
Oyasuminasai Minasan
Oyasuminasai.

Goodnight My Friends
Goodnight, my friends, goodnight
Goodnight, my friends, goodnight
Goodnight, my friends
Goodnight, my friends
Goodnight, my friends, goodnight.

にじゅうきゅう
nijuu-kyuu

29

いろ (iro)

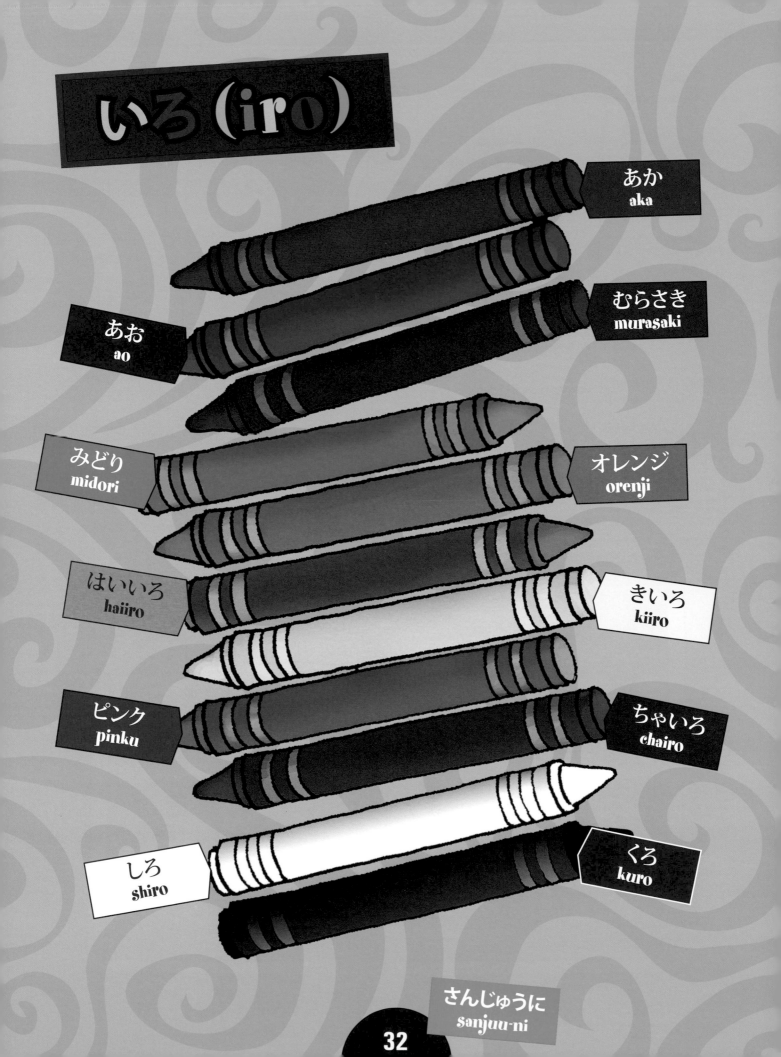

あか
aka

むらさき
murasaki

あお
ao

みどり
midori

オレンジ
orenji

はいいろ
haiiro

きいろ
kiiro

ピンク
pinku

ちゃいろ
chairo

しろ
shiro

くろ
kuro